P9-DHJ-730

A MIDSUMMER NIGHT'S DREAM

William Shakespeare

SPARK PUBLISHING

© 2002, 2007 by Spark Publishing, A Division of Barnes & Noble

This Spark Publishing edition 2014 by SparkNotes LLC, an Affiliate of Barnes & Noble

All rights reserved. No part of this publication may be reproduced, stored in a
retrieval system, or transmitted in any form or by any means (including electronic,
mechanical, photocopying, recording, or otherwise) without prior written permission
from the publisher.

122 Fifth Avenue
New York, NY 10011
www.sparknotes.com

ISBN 978-1-4114-6961-7

Please submit changes or report errors to www.sparknotes.com/errors.

Printed in Canada

10 9 8 7 6 5 4 3 2

CONTENTS

CONTEXT

THE MOST INFLUENTIAL WRITER in all of English literature, William Shakespeare was born in 1564 to a successful middle-class glove-maker in Stratford-upon-Avon, England. Shakespeare attended grammar school, but his formal education proceeded no further. In 1582 he married an older woman, Anne Hathaway, and had three children with her. Around 1590 he left his family behind and traveled to London to work as an actor and playwright. Public and critical success quickly followed, and Shakespeare eventually became the most popular playwright in England and part-owner of the Globe Theater. His career bridged the reigns of Elizabeth I (ruled 1558–1603) and James I (ruled 1603–1625), and he was a favorite of both monarchs. Indeed, James granted Shakespeare's company the greatest possible compliment by bestowing upon its members the title of King's Men. Wealthy and renowned, Shakespeare retired to Stratford and died in 1616 at the age of fifty-two. At the time of Shakespeare's death, literary luminaries such as Ben Jonson hailed his works as timeless.

Shakespeare's works were collected and printed in various editions in the century following his death, and by the early eighteenth century his reputation as the greatest poet ever to write in English was well established. The unprecedented admiration garnered by his works led to a fierce curiosity about Shakespeare's life, but the dearth of biographical information has left many details of Shakespeare's personal history shrouded in mystery. Some people have concluded from this fact that Shakespeare's plays were really written by someone else—Francis Bacon and the Earl of Oxford are the two most popular candidates—but the support for this claim is overwhelmingly circumstantial, and the theory is not taken seriously by many scholars.

In the absence of credible evidence to the contrary, Shakespeare must be viewed as the author of the thirty-seven plays and 154 sonnets that bear his name. The legacy of this body of work is immense. A number of Shakespeare's plays seem to have transcended even the category of brilliance, becoming so influential as to profoundly affect the course of Western literature and culture ever after.

Written in the mid-1590s, probably shortly before Shakespeare turned to *Romeo and Juliet*, *A Midsummer Night's Dream* is one of his strangest and most delightful creations, and it marks a departure from his earlier works and from others of the English Renaissance. The play demonstrates both the extent of Shakespeare's learning and the expansiveness of his imagination. The range of references in the play is among its most extraordinary attributes: Shakespeare draws on sources as various as Greek mythology (Theseus, for instance, is loosely based on the Greek hero of the same name, and the play is peppered with references to Greek gods and goddesses); English country fairy lore (the character of Puck, or Robin Goodfellow, was a popular figure in sixteenth-century stories); and the theatrical practices of Shakespeare's London (the craftsmen's play refers to and parodies many conventions of English Renaissance theater, such as men playing the roles of women). Further, many of the characters are drawn from diverse texts: Titania comes from Ovid's *Metamorphoses*, and Oberon may have been taken from the medieval romance *Huan of Bordeaux*, translated by Lord Berners in the mid-1530s. Unlike the plots of many of Shakespeare's plays, however, the story in *A Midsummer Night's Dream* seems not to have been drawn from any particular source but rather to be the original product of the playwright's imagination.

PLOT OVERVIEW

THESEUS, DUKE OF ATHENS, is preparing for his marriage to Hippolyta, queen of the Amazons, with a four-day festival of pomp and entertainment. He commissions his Master of the Revels, Philostrate, to find suitable amusements for the occasion. Egeus, an Athenian nobleman, marches into Theseus's court with his daughter, Hermia, and two young men, Demetrius and Lysander. Egeus wishes Hermia to marry Demetrius (who loves Hermia), but Hermia is in love with Lysander and refuses to comply. Egeus asks for the full penalty of law to fall on Hermia's head if she flouts her father's will. Theseus gives Hermia until his wedding to consider her options, warning her that disobeying her father's wishes could result in her being sent to a convent or even executed. Nonetheless, Hermia and Lysander plan to escape Athens the following night and marry in the house of Lysander's aunt, some seven leagues distant from the city. They make their intentions known to Hermia's friend Helena, who was once engaged to Demetrius and still loves him even though he jilted her after meeting Hermia. Hoping to regain his love, Helena tells Demetrius of the elopement that Hermia and Lysander have planned. At the appointed time, Demetrius stalks into the woods after his intended bride and her lover; Helena follows behind him.

In these same woods are two very different groups of characters. The first is a band of fairies, including Oberon, the fairy king, and Titania, his queen, who has recently returned from India to bless the marriage of Theseus and Hippolyta. The second is a band of Athenian craftsmen rehearsing a play that they hope to perform for the duke and his bride. Oberon and Titania are at odds over a young Indian prince given to Titania by the prince's mother; the boy is so beautiful that Oberon wishes to make him a knight, but Titania refuses. Seeking revenge, Oberon sends his merry servant, Puck, to acquire a magical flower, the juice of which can be spread over a sleeping person's eyelids to make that person fall in love with the first thing he or she sees upon waking. Puck obtains the flower, and Oberon tells him of his plan to spread its juice on the sleeping Titania's eyelids. Having seen Demetrius act cruelly toward Helena, he orders Puck to spread some of the juice on the eyelids of the young

Athenian man. Puck encounters Lysander and Hermia; thinking that Lysander is the Athenian of whom Oberon spoke, Puck afflicts him with the love potion. Lysander happens to see Helena upon awaking and falls deeply in love with her, abandoning Hermia. As the night progresses and Puck attempts to undo his mistake, both Lysander and Demetrius end up in love with Helena, who believes that they are mocking her. Hermia becomes so jealous that she tries to challenge Helena to a fight. Demetrius and Lysander nearly do fight over Helena's love, but Puck confuses them by mimicking their voices, leading them apart until they are lost separately in the forest.

When Titania wakes, the first creature she sees is Bottom, the most ridiculous of the Athenian craftsmen, whose head Puck has mockingly transformed into that of an ass. Titania passes a ludicrous interlude doting on the ass-headed weaver. Eventually, Oberon obtains the Indian boy, Puck spreads the love potion on Lysander's eyelids, and by morning all is well. Theseus and Hippolyta discover the sleeping lovers in the forest and take them back to Athens to be married—Demetrius now loves Helena, and Lysander now loves Hermia. After the group wedding, the lovers watch Bottom and his fellow craftsmen perform their play, a fumbling, hilarious version of the story of Pyramus and Thisbe. When the play is completed, the lovers go to bed; the fairies briefly emerge to bless the sleeping couples with a protective charm and then disappear. Only Puck remains, to ask the audience for its forgiveness and approval and to urge it to remember the play as though it had all been a dream.

CHARACTER LIST

Puck Also known as Robin Goodfellow, Puck is Oberon's jester, a mischievous fairy who delights in playing pranks on mortals. Though *A Midsummer Night's Dream* divides its action between several groups of characters, Puck is the closest thing the play has to a protagonist. His enchanting, mischievous spirit pervades the atmosphere, and his antics are responsible for many of the complications that propel the other main plots: he mistakes the young Athenians, applying the love potion to Lysander instead of Demetrius, thereby causing chaos within the group of young lovers; he also transforms Bottom's head into that of an ass.

Oberon The king of the fairies, Oberon is initially at odds with his wife, Titania, because she refuses to relinquish control of a young Indian prince whom he wants for a knight. Oberon's desire for revenge on Titania leads him to send Puck to obtain the love-potion flower that creates so much of the play's confusion and farce.

Titania The beautiful queen of the fairies, Titania resists the attempts of her husband, Oberon, to make a knight of the young Indian prince that she has been given. Titania's brief, potion-induced love for Nick Bottom, whose head Puck has transformed into that of an ass, yields the play's foremost example of the contrast motif.

Lysander A young man of Athens, in love with Hermia. Lysander's relationship with Hermia invokes the theme of love's difficulty: he cannot marry her openly because Egeus, her father, wishes her to wed Demetrius; when Lysander and Hermia run away into the forest, Lysander becomes the victim of misapplied magic and wakes up in love with Helena.

Demetrius   A young man of Athens, initially in love with Hermia and ultimately in love with Helena. Demetrius's obstinate pursuit of Hermia throws love out of balance among the quartet of Athenian youths and precludes a symmetrical two-couple arrangement.

Hermia   Egeus's daughter, a young woman of Athens. Hermia is in love with Lysander and is a childhood friend of Helena. As a result of the fairies' mischief with Oberon's love potion, both Lysander and Demetrius suddenly fall in love with Helena. Self-conscious about her short stature, Hermia suspects that Helena has wooed the men with her height. By morning, however, Puck has sorted matters out with the love potion, and Lysander's love for Hermia is restored.

Helena   A young woman of Athens, in love with Demetrius. Demetrius and Helena were once betrothed, but when Demetrius met Helena's friend Hermia, he fell in love with her and abandoned Helena. Lacking confidence in her looks, Helena thinks that Demetrius and Lysander are mocking her when the fairies' mischief causes them to fall in love with her.

Egeus   Hermia's father, who brings a complaint against his daughter to Theseus: Egeus has given Demetrius permission to marry Hermia, but Hermia, in love with Lysander, refuses to marry Demetrius. Egeus's severe insistence that Hermia either respect his wishes or be held accountable to Athenian law places him squarely outside the whimsical dream realm of the forest.

Theseus   The heroic duke of Athens, engaged to Hippolyta. Theseus represents power and order throughout the play. He appears only at the beginning and end of the story, removed from the dreamlike events of the forest.

Hippolyta   The legendary queen of the Amazons, engaged to Theseus. Like Theseus, she symbolizes order.

Nick Bottom The overconfident weaver chosen to play Pyramus in the craftsmen's play for Theseus's marriage celebration. Bottom is full of advice and self-confidence but frequently makes silly mistakes and misuses language. His simultaneous nonchalance about the beautiful Titania's sudden love for him and unawareness of the fact that Puck has transformed his head into that of an ass mark the pinnacle of his foolish arrogance.

Peter Quince A carpenter and the nominal leader of the craftsmen's attempt to put on a play for Theseus's marriage celebration. Quince is often shoved aside by the abundantly confident Bottom. During the craftsmen's play, Quince plays the Prologue.

Francis Flute The bellows-mender chosen to play Thisbe in the craftsmen's play for Theseus's marriage celebration. Forced to play a young girl in love, the bearded craftsman determines to speak his lines in a high, squeaky voice.

Robin Starveling The tailor chosen to play Thisbe's mother in the craftsmen's play for Theseus's marriage celebration. He ends up playing the part of Moonshine.

Tom Snout The tinker chosen to play Pyramus's father in the craftsmen's play for Theseus's marriage celebration. He ends up playing the part of Wall, dividing the two lovers.

Snug The joiner chosen to play the lion in the craftsmen's play for Theseus's marriage celebration. Snug worries that his roaring will frighten the ladies in the audience.

Philostrate Theseus's Master of the Revels, responsible for organizing the entertainment for the duke's marriage celebration.

Peaseblossom, Cobweb, Mote, and Mustardseed The fairies ordered by Titania to attend to Bottom after she falls in love with him.

ANALYSIS OF MAJOR CHARACTERS

PUCK

Though there is little character development in *A Midsummer Night's Dream* and no true protagonist, critics generally point to Puck as the most important character in the play. The mischievous, quick-witted sprite sets many of the play's events in motion with his magic, by means of both deliberate pranks on the human characters (transforming Bottom's head into that of an ass) and unfortunate mistakes (smearing the love potion on Lysander's eyelids instead of Demetrius's).

More important, Puck's capricious spirit, magical fancy, fun-loving humor, and lovely, evocative language permeate the atmosphere of the play. Wild contrasts, such as the implicit comparison between the rough, earthy craftsmen and the delicate, graceful fairies, dominate *A Midsummer Night's Dream*. Puck seems to illustrate many of these contrasts within his own character: he is graceful but not so saccharine as the other fairies; as Oberon's jester, he is given to a certain coarseness, which leads him to transform Bottom's head into that of an ass merely for the sake of enjoyment. He is good-hearted but capable of cruel tricks. Finally, whereas most of the fairies are beautiful and ethereal, Puck is often portrayed as somewhat bizarre looking. Indeed, another fairy mentions that some call Puck a "hobgoblin," a term whose connotations are decidedly less glamorous than those of "fairy" (II.i.40).

NICK BOTTOM

Whereas Puck's humor is often mischievous and subtle, the comedy surrounding the overconfident weaver Nick Bottom is hilariously overt. The central figure in the subplot involving the craftsmen's production of the Pyramus and Thisbe story, Bottom dominates his fellow actors with an extraordinary belief in his own abilities (he thinks he is perfect for every part in the play) and his comical incompetence (he is a terrible actor and frequently makes rhetorical and grammatical mistakes in his speech). The humor surrounding Bottom often stems from the fact that he is totally unaware of his own ridiculousness; his speeches are overdramatic and self-aggrandizing, and he seems to believe that everyone takes him as seriously as he does himself. This foolish self-importance reaches its pinnacle after Puck transforms Bottom's head into that of an ass. When Titania, whose eyes have been anointed with a love potion, falls in love with the now ass-headed Bottom, he believes that the devotion of the beautiful, magical fairy queen is nothing out of the ordinary and that all of the trappings of her affection, including having servants attend him, are his proper due. His unawareness of the fact that his head has been transformed into that of an ass parallels his inability to perceive the absurdity of the idea that Titania could fall in love with him.

HELENA

Although Puck and Bottom stand out as the most personable characters in *A Midsummer Night's Dream*, they themselves are not involved in the main dramatic events. Of the other characters, Helena, the lovesick young woman desperately in love with Demetrius, is perhaps the most fully drawn. Among the quartet of Athenian lovers, Helena is the one who thinks most about the nature of love—which makes sense, given that at the beginning of the play she is left out of the love triangle involving Lysander, Hermia, and Demetrius. She says, "Love looks not with the eyes, but with the mind," believing that Demetrius has built up a fantastic notion of Hermia's beauty that prevents him from recognizing Helena's own beauty (I.i.234). Utterly faithful to Demetrius despite her recognition of his shortcomings, Helena sets out to win his love by telling him about the plan of Lysander and Hermia to elope into the forest. Once Helena enters the forest, many of her traits are drawn out by the confusion that the love potion engenders: compared to the other lovers, she is extremely unsure of herself, worrying about her appearance and believing that Lysander is mocking her when he declares his love for her.

CHARACTER ANALYSIS

Themes, Symbols, & Motifs

Themes

Themes are the fundamental and often universal ideas explored in a literary work.

Love's Difficulty

"The course of true love never did run smooth," comments Lysander, articulating one of *A Midsummer Night's Dream*'s most important themes—that of the difficulty of love (I.i.134). Though most of the conflict in the play stems from the troubles of romance, and though the play involves a number of romantic elements, it is not truly a love story; it distances the audience from the emotions of the characters in order to poke fun at the torments and afflictions that those in love suffer. The tone of the play is so lighthearted that the audience never doubts that things will end happily, and it is therefore free to enjoy the comedy without being caught up in the tension of an uncertain outcome.

The theme of love's difficulty is often explored through the motif of love out of balance—that is, romantic situations in which a disparity or inequality interferes with the harmony of a relationship. The prime instance of this imbalance is the asymmetrical love among the four young Athenians: Hermia loves Lysander, Lysander loves Hermia, Helena loves Demetrius, and Demetrius loves Hermia instead of Helena—a simple numeric imbalance in which two men love the same woman, leaving one woman with too many suitors and one with too few. The play has strong potential for a traditional outcome, and the plot is in many ways based on a quest for internal balance; that is, when the lovers' tangle resolves itself into symmetrical pairings, the traditional happy ending will have been achieved. Somewhat similarly, in the relationship between Titania and Oberon, an imbalance arises out of the fact that Oberon's coveting of Titania's Indian boy outweighs his love for her. Later, Titania's passion for the ass-headed Bottom represents an imbalance of appearance and nature: Titania is beautiful and graceful, while Bottom is clumsy and grotesque.

MAGIC

The fairies' magic, which brings about many of the most bizarre and hilarious situations in the play, is another element central to the fantastic atmosphere of *A Midsummer Night's Dream*. Shakespeare uses magic both to embody the almost supernatural power of love (symbolized by the love potion) and to create a surreal world. Although the misuse of magic causes chaos, as when Puck mistakenly applies the love potion to Lysander's eyelids, magic ultimately resolves the play's tensions by restoring love to balance among the quartet of Athenian youths. Additionally, the ease with which Puck uses magic to his own ends, as when he reshapes Bottom's head into that of an ass and recreates the voices of Lysander and Demetrius, stands in contrast to the laboriousness and gracelessness of the craftsmen's attempt to stage their play.

DREAMS

As the title suggests, dreams are an important theme in *A Midsummer Night's Dream;* they are linked to the bizarre, magical mishaps in the forest. Hippolyta's first words in the play evidence the prevalence of dreams ("Four days will quickly steep themselves in night, / Four nights will quickly dream away the time"), and various characters mention dreams throughout (I.i.7–8). The theme of dreaming recurs predominantly when characters attempt to explain bizarre events in which these characters are involved: "I have had a dream, past the wit of man to say what / dream it was. Man is but an ass if he go about t'expound this dream," Bottom says, unable to fathom the magical happenings that have affected him as anything but the result of slumber.

Shakespeare is also interested in the actual workings of dreams, in how events occur without explanation, time loses its normal sense of flow, and the impossible occurs as a matter of course; he seeks to recreate this environment in the play through the intervention of the fairies in the magical forest. At the end of the play, Puck extends the idea of dreams to the audience members themselves, saying that, if they have been offended by the play, they should remember it as nothing more than a dream. This sense of illusion and gauzy fragility is crucial to the atmosphere of *A Midsummer Night's Dream*, as it helps render the play a fantastical experience rather than a heavy drama.

MOTIFS

*Motifs are recurring structures, contrasts, and literary devices
that can help to develop and inform the text's major themes.*

CONTRAST

The idea of contrast is the basic building block of *A Midsummer
Night's Dream*. The entire play is constructed around groups of opposites and doubles. Nearly every characteristic presented in the play
has an opposite: Helena is tall, Hermia is short; Puck plays pranks,
Bottom is the victim of pranks; Titania is beautiful, Bottom is grotesque. Further, the three main groups of characters (who are developed from sources as varied as Greek mythology, English folklore,
and classical literature) are designed to contrast powerfully with one
another: the fairies are graceful and magical, while the craftsmen
are clumsy and earthy; the craftsmen are merry, while the lovers are
overly serious. Contrast serves as the defining visual characteristic of
A Midsummer Night's Dream, with the play's most indelible image
being that of the beautiful, delicate Titania weaving flowers into the
hair of the ass-headed Bottom. It seems impossible to imagine two
figures less compatible with each other. The juxtaposition of extraordinary differences is the most important characteristic of the play's
surreal atmosphere and is thus perhaps the play's central motif; there
is no scene in which extraordinary contrast is not present.

SYMBOLS

*Symbols are objects, characters, figures, and colors used to
represent abstract ideas or concepts.*

THESEUS AND HIPPOLYTA

Theseus and Hippolyta bookend *A Midsummer Night's Dream*, ap-
pearing in the daylight at both the beginning and the end of the
play's main action. They disappear, however, for the duration of the
action, leaving in the middle of Act I, scene i and not reappearing
until Act IV, as the sun is coming up to end the magical night in the
forest. Shakespeare uses Theseus and Hippolyta, the ruler of Athens
and his warrior bride, to represent order and stability, to contrast
with the uncertainty, instability, and darkness of most of the play.
Whereas an important element of the dream realm is that one is not
in control of one's environment, Theseus and Hippolyta are always
entirely in control of theirs. Their reappearance in the daylight of

Act IV to hear Theseus's hounds signifies the end of the dream state of the previous night and a return to rationality.

THE LOVE POTION

The love potion is made from the juice of a flower that was struck with one of Cupid's misfired arrows; it is used by the fairies to wreak romantic havoc throughout Acts II, III, and IV. Because the meddling fairies are careless with the love potion, the situation of the young Athenian lovers becomes increasingly chaotic and confusing (Demetrius and Lysander are magically compelled to transfer their love from Hermia to Helena), and Titania is hilariously humiliated (she is magically compelled to fall deeply in love with the ass-headed Bottom). The love potion thus becomes a symbol of the unreasoning, fickle, erratic, and undeniably powerful nature of love, which can lead to inexplicable and bizarre behavior and cannot be resisted.

THE CRAFTSMEN'S PLAY

The play-within-a-play that takes up most of Act V, scene i is used to represent, in condensed form, many of the important ideas and themes of the main plot. Because the craftsmen are such bumbling actors, their performance satirizes the melodramatic Athenian lovers and gives the play a purely joyful, comedic ending. Pyramus and Thisbe face parental disapproval in the play-within-a-play, just as Hermia and Lysander do; the theme of romantic confusion enhanced by the darkness of night is rehashed, as Pyramus mistakenly believes that Thisbe has been killed by the lion, just as the Athenian lovers experience intense misery because of the mix-ups caused by the fairies' meddling. The craftsmen's play is, therefore, a kind of symbol for *A Midsummer Night's Dream* itself: a story involving powerful emotions that is made hilarious by its comical presentation.

SUMMARY & ANALYSIS

ACT I, SCENE I

SUMMARY

> *The course of true love never did run smooth....*
> *(See* QUOTATIONS, *p. 35)*

At his palace, Theseus, duke of Athens, and Hippolyta, his fiancée, discuss their wedding, to be held in four days, under the new moon. Impatient for the event and in a celebratory mood, Theseus orders Philostrate, his Master of the Revels, to "stir up the Athenian youth to merriments" and devise entertainments with which the couple might pass the time until their wedding (I.i.12). Philostrate takes his leave, and Theseus promises Hippolyta that though he wooed her with his sword (Hippolyta, queen of the Amazons, presumably met Theseus in combat), he will wed her "with pomp, with triumph, and with revelling"—with a grand celebration to begin at once and last until the wedding (I.i.19).

Egeus, a citizen of Athens, strides into the room, followed by his daughter Hermia and the Athenian youths Lysander and Demetrius. Egeus has come to see Theseus with a complaint against his daughter: although Egeus has promised her in marriage to Demetrius, who loves her, Lysander has won Hermia's heart, and Hermia refuses to obey her father and marry Demetrius. Egeus demands that the law punish Hermia if she fails to comply with his demands. Theseus speaks to Hermia sharply, telling her to expect to be sent to a nunnery or put to death. Lysander interrupts, accusing Demetrius of being fickle in love, saying that he was once engaged to Hermia's friend Helena but abandoned her after he met Hermia. Theseus admits that he has heard this story, and he takes Egeus and Demetrius aside to discuss it. Before they go, he orders Hermia to take the time remaining before his marriage to Hippolyta to make up her mind. Theseus, Hippolyta, Egeus, and Demetrius depart, leaving Hermia alone with Lysander.

Hermia and Lysander discuss the trials that must be faced by those who are in love: "The course of true love never did run smooth," Lysander says (I.i.134). He proposes a plan: he has an aunt, wealthy and childless, who lives seven leagues from Athens and who dotes on Lysander like a son. At her house, Hermia and Lysander can be married—and, because the manor is outside of Athens, they would be free from Athenian law. Hermia is overjoyed, and they agree to travel to the house the following night.

Helena, Hermia's friend whom Demetrius jilted, enters the room, lovesick and deeply melancholy because Demetrius no longer loves her. Hermia and Lysander confide their plan to her and wish her luck with Demetrius. They depart to prepare for the following night's journey. Helena remarks to herself that she envies them their happiness. She thinks up a plan: if she tells Demetrius of the elopement that Lysander and Hermia are planning, he will be bound to follow them to the woods to try to stop them; if she then follows him into the woods, she might have a chance to win back his love.

ANALYSIS

From the outset, Shakespeare subtly portrays the lovers as a group out of balance, a motif that creates tension throughout the play. For the sake of symmetry, the audience wants the four lovers to form two couples; instead, both men love Hermia, leaving Helena out of the equation. The women are thus in nonparallel situations, adding to the sense of structural imbalance. By establishing the fact that Demetrius once loved Helena, Shakespeare suggests the possibility of a harmonious resolution to this love tangle: if Demetrius could only be made to love Helena again, then all would be well. By the end of the play, the fairies' intervention affects just such an outcome, and all *does* become well, though it is worth noting that the restoration of Demetrius's love for Helena is the result of magic rather than a natural reawakening of his feelings.

The genre of comedy surrounding the Athenian lovers is farce, in which the humor stems from exaggerated characters trying to find their way out of ludicrous situations. Shakespeare portrays the lovers as overly serious, as each is deeply and earnestly preoccupied with his or her own feelings: Helena is anxious about her looks, reacting awkwardly when Lysander calls her "fair"; Hermia later becomes self-conscious about her short stature; Demetrius is willing to see Hermia executed to prevent her from marrying another man; and Lysander seems to have cast himself as the hero of a great love story in his own mind (III.ii.188, III.ii.247). Hermia is stubborn and quarrelsome, while Helena lacks self-confidence and believes that other people mock her. The airy world of the fairies and the absurd predicaments in which the lovers find themselves once in the forest make light of the lovers' grave concerns.

> *Love looks not with the eyes, but with the mind,*
> *And therefore is winged Cupid painted blind.*
> *(See* QUOTATIONS, *p. 36)*

ACT I, SCENE II

SUMMARY

In another part of Athens, far from Theseus's palace, a group of common laborers meets at the house of Peter Quince to rehearse a play that the men hope to perform for the grand celebration preceding the wedding of Theseus and Hippolyta. Quince, a carpenter, tries to conduct the meeting, but the talkative weaver Nick Bottom continually interrupts him with advice and direction. Quince tells the group what play they are to perform: *The Most Lamentable Comedy and Most Cruel Death of Pyramus and Thisbe,* which tells the story of two lovers, separated by their parents' feud, who speak to each other at night through a hole in a wall. In the play, a lion surprises Thisbe one night and tatters her mantle before she escapes. When Pyramus finds the shredded garment, he assumes that the lion has killed Thisbe; stricken with grief, he commits suicide. When Thisbe finds Pyramus's bloody corpse, she too commits suicide. Quince assigns their parts: Bottom is to play Pyramus; Francis Flute, Thisbe; Robin Starveling, Thisbe's mother; Tom Snout, Pyramus's father; Quince himself, Thisbe's father; and Snug, the lion.

As Quince doles out the parts, Bottom often interrupts, announcing that he should be the one to play the assigned part. He says that his ability to speak in a woman's voice would make him a wonderful Thisbe and that his ability to roar would make him a wonderful lion. Quince eventually convinces him that Pyramus is the part for him, by virtue of the fact that Pyramus is supposed to be very handsome. Snug worries that he will be unable to learn the lion's part, but Quince reassures him that it will be very easy to learn, since the lion speaks no words and only growls and roars. This worries the craftsmen, who reason that if the lion frightens any of the noble ladies in the audience, they will all be executed; since they are only common laborers, they do not want to risk upsetting powerful people. Bottom says that *he* could roar as sweetly as a nightingale so as not to frighten anyone, but Quince again convinces him that he can only

SUMMARY & ANALYSIS

play Pyramus. The group disperses, agreeing to meet in the woods the following night to rehearse their play.

ANALYSIS

The most important motif in *A Midsummer Night's Dream,* and one of the most important literary techniques Shakespeare uses throughout the play, is that of contrast. The three main groups of characters are all vastly different from one another, and the styles, moods, and structures of their respective subplots also differ. It is by incorporating these contrasting realms into a single story that Shakespeare creates the play's dreamlike atmosphere. Almost diametrically opposite the beautiful, serious, and love-struck young nobles are the clumsy, ridiculous, and deeply confused craftsmen, around whom many of the play's most comical scenes are centered.

Where the young lovers are graceful and well spoken—almost comically well suited to their roles as melodramatically passionate youths—the craftsmen often fumble their words and could not be less well suited for acting. This disjunction reveals itself as it becomes readily apparent that the craftsmen have no idea how to put on a dramatic production: their speeches are full of impossible ideas and mistakes (Bottom, for example, claims that he will roar "as gently / as any sucking dove"); their concerns about their parts are absurd (Flute does not want to play Thisbe because he is growing a beard); and their extended discussion about whether they will be executed if the lion's roaring frightens the ladies further evidences the fact that their primary concern is with themselves, not their art (II.i.67–68).

The fact that the workmen have chosen to perform the Pyramus and Thisbe story, a Babylonian myth familiar to Shakespeare's audiences from Ovid's *Metamorphoses,* only heightens the comedy. The story of Pyramus and Thisbe is highly dramatic, with suicides and tragically wasted love (themes that Shakespeare takes up in *Romeo and Juliet* as well). Badly suited to their task and inexperienced, although endlessly well meaning, the craftsmen are sympathetic figures even when the audience laughs at them—a fact made explicit in Act V, when Theseus makes fun of their play even as he honors their effort. The contrast between the serious nature of the play and the bumbling foolishness of the craftsmen makes the endeavor all the more ridiculous. Further, the actors' botched telling of the youthful love between Pyramus and Thisbe implicitly mocks the melodramatic love tangle of Hermia, Helena, Demetrius, and Lysander.

ACT II, SCENE I

SUMMARY

In the forest, two fairies, one a servant of Titania, the other a servant of Oberon, meet by chance in a glade. Oberon's servant tells Titania's to be sure to keep Titania out of Oberon's sight, for the two are very angry with each other. Titania, he says, has taken a little Indian prince as her attendant, and the boy is so beautiful that Oberon wishes to make him his knight. Titania, however, refuses to give the boy up.

Titania's servant is delighted to recognize Oberon's servant as Robin Goodfellow, better known as Puck, a mischievous sprite notorious for his pranks and jests. Puck admits his identity and describes some of the tricks he plays on mortals.

The two are interrupted when Oberon enters from one side of the glade, followed by a train of attendants. At the same moment, Titania enters from the other side of the glade, followed by her own train. The two fairy royals confront one another, each questioning the other's motive for coming so near to Athens just before the marriage of Theseus and Hippolyta. Titania accuses Oberon of loving Hippolyta and of thus wishing to bless the marriage; Oberon accuses Titania of loving Theseus. The conversation turns to the little Indian boy, whom Oberon asks Titania to give him. But Titania responds that the boy's mother was a devotee of hers before she died; in honor of his mother's memory, Titania will hold the boy near to her. She invites Oberon to go with her to dance in a fairy round and see her nightly revels, but Oberon declines, saying that they will be at odds until she gives him the boy.

Titania storms away, and Oberon vows to take revenge on her before the night is out. He sends Puck to seek a white-and-purple flower called love-in-idleness, which was once hit with one of Cupid's arrows. He says that the flower's juice, if rubbed on a sleeper's eyelids, will cause the sleeper to fall in love with the first living thing he or she sees upon waking. Oberon announces that he will use this juice on Titania, hoping that she will fall in love with some ridiculous creature; he will then refuse to lift the juice's effect until she yields the Indian prince to him.

ANALYSIS

Act II serves two main functions: it introduces the fairies and their realm, and it initiates the romantic confusion that will eventually help restore the balance of love. The fairies, whom Shakespeare bases heavily on characters familiar from English folklore, are among the most memorable and delightful characters in the play. They speak in lilting rhymes infused with gorgeous poetic imagery. *A Midsummer Night's Dream* is a play dominated by the presence of doubles, and the fairies are designed to contrast heavily with the young lovers and the craftsmen. Whereas the lovers are earnest and serious, Puck and the other pixies are merry and full of laughter; whereas the craftsmen are bumbling, earthy, and engage in methodical labor, the fairies are delicate, airy, and indulge in effortless magic and enchantment.

The conflict between Oberon and Titania imports into the fairy realm the motif of love being out of balance. As with the Athenian lovers, the eventual resolution of the tension between the two occurs only by means of magic. Though the craftsmen do not experience romantic confusion about one another, Bottom becomes involved in an accidental romance with Titania in Act III, and in Act V two craftsmen portray the lovers Pyramus and Thisbe, who commit suicide after misinterpreting events.

A Midsummer Night's Dream was probably performed before Queen Elizabeth, and Shakespeare managed to make a flattering reference to his monarch in Act II, scene i. When Oberon introduces the idea of the love potion to Puck, he says that he once saw Cupid fire an arrow that missed its mark:

> *That very time I saw, but thou couldst not,*
> *Flying between the cold moon and the earth*
> *Cupid, all armed.*
> *A certain aim he took*
> *At a fair vestal thronèd by the west,*
> *And loosed his love-shaft smartly from his bow*
> *As it should pierce a hundred thousand hearts.*
> *But I might see young Cupid's fiery shaft*
> *Quenched in the chaste beams of the wat'ry moon,*
> *And the imperial vot'ress passèd on,*
> *In maiden meditation, fancy-free*
>
> *(II.i.155–164).*

Queen Elizabeth never married and was celebrated in her time as a woman of chastity, a virgin queen whose concerns were above the flesh. Here Shakespeare alludes to that reputation by describing Cupid firing an arrow "at a fair vestal thronèd by the west"— Queen Elizabeth—whom the heat of passion cannot affect because

SUMMARY & ANALYSIS

the arrow is cooled "in the chaste beams of the wat'ry moon." Shakespeare celebrates how Elizabeth put affairs of state before her personal life and lived "in maiden meditation, fancy-free." He nestles a patriotic aside in an evocative description, couching praise for the ruler on whose good favor he depended in dexterous poetic language. (Audiences in Shakespeare's day would most likely have recognized this imaginative passage's reference to their monarch.)

Because many of the main themes and motifs in *A Midsummer Night's Dream* are very light, even secondary to the overall sense of comedy and the dreamlike atmosphere, it is perhaps more important to try to understand not *what* the play means but rather *how* Shakespeare creates its mood. One technique that he uses is to embellish action with a wealth of finely wrought poetic imagery, using language to work upon the imagination of the audience and thereby affect a kind of magic upon the stage: "I must go seek some dewdrops here," one fairy says, "And hang a pearl in every cowslip's ear" (II.i.14–15). The fairies conjure many of the play's most evocative images: Oberon, for instance, describes having heard

> *a mermaid on a dolphin's back*
> *Uttering such dulcet and harmonious breath*
> *That the rude sea grew civil at her song*
> *And certain stars shot madly from their spheres*
> *To hear the sea-maid's music*
>
> *(II.i.150–154)*

and seen

> *a bank where the wild thyme blows,*
> *Where oxlips and the nodding violet grows,*
> *Quite overcanopied with luscious woodbine,*
> *With sweet musk-roses, and with eglantine.*
> *There sleeps Titania sometime of the night,*
> *Lulled in these flowers with dances and delight*
> *(II.i.249–254).*

This technique extends even to the suggestive names of some of the characters, such as the craftsmen Snug, Starveling, Quince, Flute, and Snout and the fairies Cobweb, Mustardseed, Mote, and Peaseblossom.

Act II, scene ii

Summary

As Puck flies off to seek the flower, Demetrius and Helena pass through the glade. Oberon makes himself invisible so that he can watch and hear them. Demetrius harangues Helena, saying that he does not love her, does not want to see her, and wishes that she would stop following him immediately. He curses Lysander and Hermia, whom he is pursuing, hoping to prevent their marriage and slay Lysander. Helena repeatedly declares her adoration for, and loyalty to, Demetrius, who repeatedly insults her. They exit the grove, with Helena following closely behind Demetrius, and Oberon materializes. He declares that before the night is out, Demetrius will be the one chasing Helena.

Puck appears, carrying the flower whose juice will serve as the love potion. Oberon takes the flower and says that he knows of a fragrant stream bank surrounded with flowers where Titania often sleeps. Before hurrying away to anoint Titania's eyelids with the flower's juice, Oberon orders Puck to look for an Athenian youth being pursued by a lady and to put some of the juice on the disdainful youth's eyelids, so that when he wakes he will fall in love with the lady. He informs Puck that he will know the youth by his Athenian garb. Puck agrees to carry out his master's wishes.

After her dancing and revelry, Titania falls asleep by the stream bank. Oberon creeps up on her and squeezes the flower's juice onto her eyelids so that Titania will fall in love with the first creature she sees upon waking. Oberon departs, and Lysander and Hermia wander into the glade. Lysander admits that he has forgotten the way to his aunt's house and says that they should sleep in the forest until morning, when they can find their way by daylight. Lysander wishes to sleep close to Hermia, but she insists that they sleep apart, to respect custom and propriety. At some distance from each other, they fall asleep.

Puck enters, complaining that he has looked everywhere but cannot find an Athenian youth and pursuing lady. He is relieved when he finally happens upon the sleeping forms of Lysander and Hermia, assuming that they are the Athenians of whom Oberon spoke. Noticing that the two are sleeping apart, Puck surmises that the youth refused to let Hermia come closer to him. Calling him a "churl," Puck spreads the potion on Lysander's eyelids, and he departs.

SUMMARY & ANALYSIS

Simultaneously, Helena pursues Demetrius through the glade. He insults her again and insists that she no longer follow him. She complains that she is afraid of the dark, but he nonetheless storms off without her. Saying that she is out of breath, Helena remains behind, bemoaning her unrequited love. She sees the sleeping Lysander and wakes him up. The potion takes effect, and Lysander falls deeply in love with Helena. He begins to praise her beauty and to declare his undying passion for her. Disbelieving, Helena reminds him that he loves Hermia; he declares that Hermia is nothing to him. Helena believes that Lysander is making fun of her, and she grows angry. She leaves in a huff, and Lysander follows after her. Hermia soon wakes and is shocked to find that Lysander is gone. She stumbles into the woods to find him.

ANALYSIS

Act II, scene ii introduces the plot device of the love potion, which Shakespeare uses to explore the comic possibilities inherent in the motif of love out of balance. Oberon's meddling in the affairs of humans further disrupts the love equilibrium, and the love potion symbolizes the fact that the lovers themselves will not reason out their dilemmas; rather, an outside force—magic—will resolve the love tangle.

The ease with which characters' affections change in the play, so that Lysander is madly in love with Hermia at one point and with Helena at another, has troubled some readers, who feel that Shakespeare profanes the idea of true love by treating it as inconstant and subject to outside manipulation. It is important to remember, however, that while *A Midsummer Night's Dream* contains elements of romance, it is not a true love story like *Romeo and Juliet.* Shakespeare's aim is not to comment on the nature of true love but rather to mock gently the melodramatic afflictions and confusions that love induces. Demetrius, Helena, Hermia, and Lysander are meant not to be romantic archetypes but rather sympathetic figures thrown into the confusing circumstances of a romantic farce.

Like much farce, *A Midsummer Night's Dream* relies heavily on misunderstanding and mistaken identity to create its humorous entanglements. Oberon's unawareness of the presence of a second Athenian couple—Lysander and Hermia—in the forest enables Puck's mistaken application of the flower's juice. This confusion underscores the crucial role of circumstance in the play: it is not people who are responsible for what happens but rather fate. In

Hamlet and *Macbeth,* oppositely, Shakespeare forces his characters to make crucial decisions that affect their lives.

Much of the comic tension in this scene (and throughout the rest of the play, as the confusion wrought by the love potion only increases) stems from the fact that the solution to the love tangle seems so simple to the reader/audience: if Demetrius could simply be made to love Hermia, then the lovers could pair off symmetrically, and love would be restored to a point of balance. Shakespeare teases the audience by dangling the magic flower as a simple mechanism by which this resolution could be achieved. He uses this mechanism, however, to cycle through a number of increasingly ridiculous arrangements before he allows the love story to arrive at its inevitable happy conclusion.

Act III, scene i

Summary

The craftsmen meet in the woods at the appointed time to rehearse their play. Since they will be performing in front of a large group of nobles (and since they have an exaggerated sense of the delicacy of noble ladies), Bottom declares that certain elements of the play must be changed. He fears that Pyramus's suicide and the lion's roaring will frighten the ladies and lead to the actors' executions. The other men share Bottom's concern, and they decide to write a prologue explaining that the lion is not *really* a lion nor the sword *really* a sword and assuring the ladies that no one will *really* die. They decide also that, to clarify the fact that the story takes place at night and that Pyramus and Thisbe are separated by a wall, one man must play the wall and another the moonlight by carrying a bush and a lantern.

As the craftsmen rehearse, Puck enters and marvels at the scene of the "hempen homespuns" trying to act (III.i.65). When Bottom steps aside, temporarily out of view of the other craftsmen, Puck transforms Bottom's head into that of an ass. When the ass-headed Bottom reenters the scene, the other men become terrified and run for their lives. Delighting in the mischief, Puck chases after them. Bottom, perplexed, remains behind.

In the same grove, the sleeping Titania wakes. When she sees Bottom, the flower juice on her eyelids works its magic, and she falls deeply and instantly in love with the ass-headed weaver. She insists that he remain with her, embraces him, and appoints a group of fairies—Peaseblossom, Cobweb, Mote, and Mustardseed—to see to his

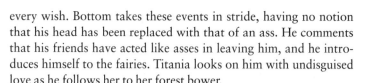

every wish. Bottom takes these events in stride, having no notion that his head has been replaced with that of an ass. He comments that his friends have acted like asses in leaving him, and he introduces himself to the fairies. Titania looks on him with undisguised love as he follows her to her forest bower.

ANALYSIS

The structure of *A Midsummer Night's Dream* is roughly such that Act I introduces the main characters and the conflict; Act II sets up the interaction among the Athenian lovers, the fairies, and the craftsmen (the lovers wander through the forest, the fairies make mischief with the love potion); and Act III develops the comical possibilities of these interactions. As Act III is the first act in which all three groups appear, the fantastic contrasts between them are at their most visible.

The craftsmen's attempt at drama is a comedy of incongruity, as the rough, unsophisticated men demonstrate their utter inability to conceive a competent theatrical production. Their proposal to let the audience know that it is night by having a character play the role of Moonshine exemplifies their straightforward, literal manner of thinking and their lack of regard for subtlety. In their earthy and practical natures, the craftsmen stand in stark contrast to the airy and impish fairies.

The fairies' magic is one of the main components of the dreamlike atmosphere of *A Midsummer Night's Dream,* and it is integral to the plot's progression. It throws love increasingly out of balance and brings the farce into its most frenzied state. With the youths' love tangle already affected by the potion, Shakespeare creates further havoc by generating a romance across groups, as Titania falls in love with the ass-headed Bottom. Obviously, the delicate fairy queen is dramatically unsuited to the clumsy, monstrous craftsman. Shakespeare develops this romance with fantastic aplomb and heightens the comedy of the incongruity by making Bottom fully unaware of his transformed state. Rather, Bottom is so self-confident that he finds it fairly unremarkable that the beautiful fairy queen should wish desperately to become his lover. Further, his ironic reference to his colleagues as asses and his hunger for hay emphasize the ridiculousness of his lofty self-estimation.

ACT III, SCENES II–III

SUMMARY: ACT III, SCENE I

> *Lord, what fools these mortals be!*
> *(See* QUOTATIONS, *p. 37)*

In another part of the forest, Puck tells Oberon about the predicament involving Titania and Bottom. Oberon is delighted that his plan is working so well. Hermia, having discovered Demetrius after losing Lysander, enters the clearing with Demetrius. Puck is surprised to see the woman he saw earlier with a different man from the one he enchanted. Oberon is surprised to see the man he ordered Puck to enchant with a different woman. He realizes that a mistake has been made and says that he and Puck will have to remedy it. Hermia presses Demetrius about Lysander's whereabouts, fearing that he is dead, but Demetrius does not know where Lysander has gone, and he is bitter and reproachful that Hermia would rather be with Lysander than with him. Hermia grows angrier and angrier, and Demetrius decides that it is pointless to follow her. He lies down and falls asleep, and Hermia stalks away to find Lysander.

When Hermia is gone, Oberon sends Puck to find Helena and squeezes the flower juice onto Demetrius's eyelids. Puck quickly returns, saying that Helena is close behind him. Helena enters with Lysander still pledging his undying love to her. Still believing that he is mocking her, Helena remains angry and hurt. The noise of their bickering wakes Demetrius, who sees Helena and immediately falls in love with her. Demetrius joins Lysander in declaring this love. Lysander argues that Demetrius does not really love Helena; Demetrius argues that Lysander is truly in love with Hermia. Helena believes that they are both mocking her and refuses to believe that either one loves her.

Hermia reenters, having heard Lysander from a distance. When she learns that her beloved Lysander now claims to love Helena, as does Demetrius, she is appalled and incredulous. Helena, who is likewise unable to fathom that both men could be in love with her, assumes that Hermia is involved in the joke that she believes the men are playing on her, and she chides Hermia furiously for treating their friendship so lightly. Lysander and Demetrius are ready to fight one another for Helena's love; as they lunge at one another, Hermia holds Lysander back, provoking his scorn and disgust: "I will shake thee from me like a serpent" (III.ii.262). Hermia begins to suspect that

Helena has somehow acted to steal Lysander's love from her, and she surmises that, because she is short and Helena is tall, Helena must have used her height to lure Lysander. She grows furious with Helena and threatens to scratch out her eyes. Helena becomes afraid, saying that Hermia was always much quicker than she to fight. Demetrius and Lysander vow to protect Helena from Hermia, but they quickly become angry with each other and storm off into the forest to have a duel. Helena runs away from Hermia, and Hermia, reannouncing her amazement at the turn of events, departs.

Oberon dispatches Puck to prevent Lysander and Demetrius from fighting and says that they must resolve this confusion by morning. Puck flies through the forest hurling insults in the voices of both Lysander and Demetrius, confusing the would-be combatants until they are hopelessly lost.

SUMMARY: ACT III, SCENE III

Eventually, all four of the young Athenian lovers wander back separately into the glade and fall asleep. Puck squeezes the love potion onto Lysander's eyelids, declaring that in the morning all will be well.

ANALYSIS

The confusion in Act III continues to heighten, as the Athenian lovers and the fairies occupy the stage simultaneously, often without seeing each other. The comedy is at its silliest, and the characters are at their most extreme: Helena and Hermia nearly come to blows as a result of their physical insecurities, and Lysander and Demetrius actually try to have a duel. The plot is at its most chaotic, and, though there is no real climax in *A Midsummer Night's Dream,* the action is at its most intense. With the falling action of Acts IV and V, however, matters will sort themselves out quickly and order will be restored.

Like Act III, scene i, Act III, scene ii serves a mainly developmental role in the plot structure of *A Midsummer Night's Dream,* focusing on the increasing confusion among the four Athenian lovers. Now that both men have been magically induced to switch their love from Hermia to Helena, the vanities and insecurities of both women become far more pronounced. Helena's low self-esteem prevents her from believing that either man could really be in love with her. Hermia, who is used to having both men fawn on her, has her vanity stung by the fact that they are suddenly cold and indifferent toward her. She reveals a latent insecurity about her short stature when she assumes that Helena has used her height ("her personage, her tall personage") to win Lysander's love, and her quick temper is revealed in Helena's fear that Hermia will attack her (III.ii.293). The men's exaggerated masculine aggression leads them to vow to protect Helena from the dreaded Hermia—a ridiculous state of affairs given that they are two armed men whereas Hermia is a tiny, unarmed woman. Their aggression betrays Helena, however, as the men refocus it on their competition for her love.

The potion is responsible for the confusion of the lovers' situation; thus, Shakespeare links the theme of magic to the motif of imbalanced love, which dominates the scene. Had the love potion never been brought into play, the Athenian lovers would still be tangled in their romantic mess, but they would all understand it, whereas the fairies' meddling has left both Hermia and Helena unable to comprehend the situation. Additionally, Puck's magical ventriloquism is what prevents Lysander and Demetrius from killing each other at the end of the scene. Thus, magic both brings about their mutual hostility (to this point, Lysander has not been antagonistic toward Demetrius) and resolves it.

ACT IV, SCENE I

SUMMARY

> [M]an's hand is not able to taste, his tongue to
> conceive, nor his heart to report what my dream was.
> (See QUOTATIONS, p. 38)

As the Athenian lovers lie asleep in the grove, Titania enters with Bottom, still with the head of an ass, and their fairy attendants. Titania tells Bottom to lie down with his head in her lap, so that she may twine roses into his hair and kiss his "fair large ears" (IV.i.4). Bottom orders Peaseblossom to scratch his head and sends Cobweb to find him some honey. Titania asks Bottom if he is hungry, and he replies that he has a strange appetite for hay. Titania suggests that she send a fairy to fetch him nuts from a squirrel's hoard, but Bottom says that he would rather have a handful of dried peas. Yawning, he declares that he is very tired. Titania tells him to sleep in her arms, and she sends the fairies away. Gazing at Bottom's head, she cries, "O how I love thee, how I dote on thee!" and they fall asleep (IV.i.42).

Puck and Oberon enter the glade and comment on the success of Oberon's revenge. Oberon says that he saw Titania earlier in the woods and taunted her about her love for the ass-headed Bottom;

he asked her for the Indian child, promising to undo the spell if she would yield him, to which she consented. Satisfied, Oberon bends over the sleeping Titania and speaks the charm to undo the love potion. Titania wakes and is amazed to find that she is sleeping with the donkeylike Bottom. Oberon calls for music and takes his queen away to dance. She says that she hears the morning lark, and they exit. Puck speaks a charm over Bottom to restore his normal head, and he follows after his master.

As dawn breaks, Theseus, his attendants, Hippolyta, and Egeus enter to hear the baying of Theseus's hounds. They are startled to find the Athenian youths sleeping in the glade. They wake them and demand their story, which the youths are only partly able to recall—to them, the previous night seems as insubstantial as a dream. All that is clear to them is that Demetrius and Helena love each other, as do Lysander and Hermia. Theseus orders them to follow him to the temple for a great wedding feast. As they leave, Bottom wakes. He says that he has had a wondrous dream and that he will have Peter Quince write a ballad of his dream to perform at the end of their play.

ANALYSIS

Barely 300 lines long, Act IV is the shortest and most transitional of *A Midsummer Night's Dream*'s five acts. The first three serve respectively to introduce the characters, establish the comic situation, and develop the comedy; Act IV ends the conflict and leads to the happy ending in Act V. What is most remarkable, perhaps, is the speed with which the conflict is resolved and the farce comes to an end; despite the ubiquity of chaos in Act III, all that is necessary to resolve matters is a bit of potion on Lysander's eyelids and Oberon's forgiveness of his wife. The climactic moment between Titania and Oberon, during which she agrees to give him the Indian boy, is not even shown onstage but is merely described.

Though Demetrius's love of Helena is a by-product of the magic potion rather than an expression of his natural feelings, love has been put into balance, allowing for a traditional marriage ending. As is often the case with Shakespeare, the dramatic situation is closely tied to the circumstances of the external environment; just as the conflict is ending and a semblance of order is restored among the characters, the sun comes up. There is no real climax in *A Midsummer Night's Dream;* rather, as soon as the scenario has progressed to a suitable degree of complication and hilarity, Shakespeare simply invokes the fairies' magic to dispel all conflict. As the sun comes up, the reappearance of Theseus and Hippolyta, who symbolize the power and structure of the outside world, begins to dispel the magical dream of the play.

Theseus and Hippolyta bookend the play. They are extremely important figures both at its beginning and at its end, but they disappear entirely during the main action in the magical forest. The duke and his Amazon bride are romanticized in the play, but they belong solely to the nonmagical waking world, where they remain wholly in control of their own feelings and actions. An important element of the dream realm, as the lovers come to realize upon waking in a daze, is that one is in control of neither oneself nor one's surroundings. In this way, the forest and fairies contribute to the lovers' sense of their experience as a dream, even though the action happens largely while they are awake.

ACT IV, SCENE II

SUMMARY

At Quince's house, the craftsmen sit somberly and worry about their missing friend Bottom. Having last seen him shortly before the appearance of the ass-headed monster in the forest, the craftsmen worry that he has been felled by this terrifying creature. Starveling suspects that the fairies have cast some enchantment on Bottom. Flute asks whether they will go through with the play if Bottom does not return from the woods, and Peter Quince declares that to do so would be impossible, as Bottom is the only man in Athens capable of portraying Pyramus. The sad craftsmen agree that their friend is the wittiest, most intelligent, and best person in all of Athens.

Snug enters with an alarming piece of news: Theseus has been married, along with "two or three lords and ladies" (presumably Lysander, Hermia, Demetrius, and Helena), and the newlyweds are eager to see a play (IV.ii.16). Flute laments Bottom's absence, noting that Bottom would certainly have won a great deal of money from the admiring duke for his portrayal of Pyramus.

Just then, Bottom bursts triumphantly into the room and asks why everyone looks so sad. The men are overjoyed to see him, and he declares that he has an amazing story to tell them about his adventure in the forest. Quince asks to hear it, but Bottom says that there is no time: they must don their costumes and go straight to the duke's palace to perform their play. As they leave, Bottom tells them not to eat onions or garlic before the play, as they must be prepared to "utter sweet breath" (IV.ii.36).

ANALYSIS

This brief comic scene returns the focus of the play to the subplot of the Athenian craftsmen. Structurally, Act IV, scene ii represents something of a new beginning for *A Midsummer Night's Dream:* the main conflict of the play has been resolved, but rather than ending with the weddings of the lovers, as is customary in an Elizabethan comedy (the weddings do not even occur onstage here), Shakespeare chooses to include an extended epilogue devoted to sheer comedy. The epilogue takes up all of Act V and centers around the craftsmen's performance of *Pyramus and Thisbe* for the Athenian crowd. Act IV, scene ii transfers the focus of the play from magic and unbalanced love to a play-within-a-play, in which the themes of *A Midsummer Night's Dream,* not too heavy to begin with, are recycled into a form so ridiculous and garbled that the play draws to a wholly untroubled conclusion.

Though the preceding events of *A Midsummer Night's Dream* have been far from tragic, many of the characters have experienced unpleasant emotions, such as jealousy, lovesickness, and insecurity. Act IV, scene ii makes a basic transition from sadness to joy as Bottom's return transforms his fellow craftsmen's sorrow and confusion into delight and eagerness. It is no coincidence that Bottom's reappearance occurs almost simultaneously with the audience being told that the lovers have been married. Just as the marriages dispel the romantic angst of the play, so does Bottom's return dispel the worry of his comrades. Similarly, the arrival in the forest of Theseus and Hippolyta, representatives of order, coincides with the Athenian lovers' waking from their chaotic, dreamlike romp of the previous night.

ACT V, SCENES I–EPILOGUE

SUMMARY: ACT V, SCENE I

At his palace, Theseus speaks with Hippolyta about the story that the Athenian youths have told them concerning the magical romantic mix-ups of the previous night. Theseus says that he does not believe the story, adding that darkness and love have a way of exciting the imagination. Hippolyta notes, however, that if their story is not true, then it is quite strange that all of the lovers managed to narrate the events in exactly the same way.

The youths enter and Theseus greets them heartily. He says that they should pass the time before bed with a performance, and he summons Egeus (or, in some editions of *A Midsummer Night's Dream,* Philostrate) to read him a list of plays, each of which Theseus deems unacceptable. Egeus then tells him of the Pyramus and Thisbe story that the common craftsmen have prepared; warning that it is terrible in every respect, he urges Theseus not to see it. Theseus, however, says that if the craftsmen's intentions are dutiful, there will be something of merit in the play no matter how poor the performance.

The lords and ladies take their seats, and Quince enters to present a prologue, which he speaks haltingly. His strange pauses put the meaning of his words in question, so that he says, "Our true intent is. All for your delight / We are not here. That you should here repent you," though he means to communicate that "Our true intent is all for your delight. / We are not here that you should here repent you" (V.i.114–115). The other players then enter, including two characters performing the roles of Wall and Moonshine. They act out a clumsy version of the story, during which the noblemen and women joke among themselves about the actors' strange speeches and misapprehensions. Bottom, in particular, makes many perplexing statements while playing Pyramus, such as "I see a voice...I can hear my Thisbe's face" (V.i.190–191). Pyramus and Thisbe meet at, and speak across, the actor playing Wall, who holds up his fingers to indicate a chink. Snug, as the lion, enters and pours forth a speech explaining to the ladies that he is not really a lion. He roars, scaring Thisbe away, and clumsily rends her mantle. Finding the bloody mantle, Pyramus duly commits suicide. Thisbe does likewise when she finds her Pyramus dead. After the conclusion of the play, during which Bottom pretends to kill himself, with a cry of "die, die, die, die, die," Bottom asks if the audience would like an epilogue or a bergamask dance; Theseus replies that they will see the dance (V.i.295). Bottom and Flute perform the dance, and the whole group exits for bed.

Summary: Act V, scene ii–epilogue

Think but this, and all is mended:
That you have but slumbered here,
While these visions did appear.

(See QUOTATIONS, *p. 39)*

Puck enters and says that, now that night has fallen, the fairies will
come to the castle and that he has been "sent with broom before / To
sweep the dust behind the door" (V.ii.19–20). Oberon and Titania
enter and bless the palace and its occupants with a fairy song, so
that the lovers will always be true to one another, their children will
be beautiful, and no harm will ever visit Theseus and Hippolyta.
Oberon and Titania take their leave, and Puck makes a final address
to the audience. He says that if the play has offended, the audience should remember it simply as a dream. He wishes the audience
members good night and asks them to give him their hands in ap-
plause if they are kind friends.

Analysis

The structure of *A Midsummer Night's Dream* is somewhat com-
pacted in that the first four acts contain all of the play's main action,
with the height of conflict occurring in Act III and a happy turn of
events resembling a conclusion in Act IV. Act V serves as a kind of
joyful comic epilogue to the rest of the play, focusing on the craftsmen's hilariously bungling efforts to present their play and on the
noble Athenians' good-natured jesting during the craftsmen's performance. The heady tragedy of *Pyramus and Thisbe* becomes comical
in the hands of the craftsmen. The bearded Flute's portrayal of the
maiden Thisbe as well as the melodramatic ("Thou wall, O wall, O
sweet and lovely wall") and nonsensical ("Sweet moon, I thank thee
for thy sunny beams") language of the play strips the performance of
any seriousness or profound meaning (V.i.174, V.i.261).

The story of Pyramus and Thisbe, which comes from an ancient
Babylonian legend often reworked in European mythology, would
have been familiar to educated members of Shakespeare's audiences.
The story likely influenced *Romeo and Juliet*, although Shakespeare
also pulled elements from other versions of the Romeo and Juliet
tale. In both stories, two young lovers from feuding families communicate under cover of darkness; both male lovers erroneously
think their beloveds dead and commit suicide, and both females do
likewise when they find their lovers dead.

Insofar as the fifth act of *A Midsummer Night's Dream* has thematic significance (the main purpose of the play-within-a-play is to provide comic enjoyment), it is that the Pyramus and Thisbe story revisits the themes of romantic hardship and confusion that run through the main action of the play. Pyramus and Thisbe are kept apart by parental will, just as Lysander and Hermia were; their tragic end results from misinterpretation—Pyramus takes Thisbe's bloody mantle as proof that she is dead, which recalls, to some extent, Puck's mistaking of Lysander for Demetrius (as well as Titania's misconception of Bottom as a beautiful lover). In this way, the play-within-a-play lightheartedly satirizes the anguish that earlier plagued the Athenian lovers.

Given the title *A Midsummer Night's Dream,* it is no surprise that one of the main themes of the play is dreams, particularly as they relate to darkness and love. When morning comes, ending the magical night in the forest, the lovers begin to suspect that their experience in the woods was merely a dream. Theseus suggests as much to Hippolyta, who finds it strange that all the young lovers would have had the *same* dream. In the famous final speech of the play, Puck turns this idea outward, recommending that if audience members did not enjoy the play, they should assume that they have simply been dreaming throughout. This suggestion captures perfectly the delicate, insubstantial nature of *A Midsummer Night's Dream:* just as the fairies mended their mischief by sorting out the romantic confusion of the young lovers, Puck accounts for the whimsical nature of the play by explaining it as a manifestation of the subconscious.

Important Quotations Explained

1.   Ay me, for aught that I could ever read,
      Could ever hear by tale or history,
      The course of true love never did run smooth. . . .

Lysander speaks these lines to soothe Hermia when she despairs about the difficulties facing their love, specifically, that Egeus, her father, has forbidden them to marry and that Theseus has threatened her with death if she disobeys her father (I.i.132–134). Lysander tells Hermia that as long as there has been true love, there have been seemingly insurmountable difficulties to challenge it. He goes on to list a number of these difficulties, many of which later appear in the play: differences in birth or age ("misgrafted in respect of years") and difficulties caused by friends or "war, death, or sickness," which make love seem "swift as a shadow, short as any dream" (I.i.137, I.i.142–144). But, as Hermia comments, lovers must persevere, treating their difficulties as a price that must be paid for romantic bliss. As such, the above lines inaugurate the play's exploration of the theme of love's difficulties and presage what lies ahead for Lysander and Hermia: they will face great difficulties but will persevere and ultimately arrive at a happy ending.

2.   Through Athens I am thought as fair as she.
        But what of that? Demetrius thinks not so.
        He will not know what all but he do know.
        And as he errs, doting on Hermia's eyes,
        So I, admiring of his qualities.
        Things base and vile, holding no quantity,
        Love can transpose to form and dignity.
        Love looks not with the eyes, but with the mind,
        And therefore is winged Cupid painted blind.

Helena utters these lines as she comments on the irrational nature of love. They are extremely important to the play's overall presentation of love as erratic, inexplicable, and exceptionally powerful (I.i.227–235). Distressed by the fact that her beloved Demetrius loves Hermia and not her, Helena says that though she is as beautiful as Hermia, Demetrius cannot see her beauty. Helena adds that she dotes on Demetrius (though not all of his qualities are admirable) in the same way that he dotes on Hermia. She believes that love has the power to transform "base and vile" qualities into "form and dignity"—that is, even ugliness and bad behavior can seem attractive to someone in love. This is the case, she argues, because "love looks not with the eyes, but with the mind"—love depends not on an objective assessment of appearance but rather on an individual perception of the beloved. These lines prefigure aspects of the play's examination of love, such as Titania's passion for the ass-headed Bottom, which epitomizes the transformation of the "base and vile" into "form and dignity."

QUOTATIONS

3.   Lord, what fools these mortals be!

Puck makes this declaration in his amazement at the ludicrous behavior of the young Athenians (III.ii.115). This line is one of the
most famous in *A Midsummer Night's Dream* for its pithy humor,
but it is also thematically important: first, because it captures the exaggerated silliness of the lovers' behavior; second, because it marks
the contrast between the human lovers, completely absorbed in their
emotions, and the magical fairies, impish and never too serious.

4. I have had a most rare vision. I have had a dream past
    the wit of man to say what dream it was. Man is but an
    ass if he go about t'expound this dream. Methought I
    was—there is no man can tell what. Methought I was, and
    methought I had—but man is but a patched fool if he will
    offer to say what methought I had. The eye of man hath
    not heard, the ear of man hath not seen, man's hand is
    not able to taste, his tongue to conceive, nor his heart to
    report what my dream was. I will get Peter Quince to write
    a ballad of this dream. It shall be called 'Bottom's Dream',
    because it hath no bottom.

Bottom makes this bombastic speech after he wakes up from his
adventure with Titania; his human head restored, he believes that
his experience as an ass-headed monster beloved by the beautiful
fairy queen was merely a bizarre dream (IV.i.199–209). He remarks
dramatically that his dream is beyond human comprehension; then,
contradicting himself, he says that he will ask Quince to write a ballad about this dream. These lines are important partially because
they offer humorous commentary on the theme of dreams throughout the play but also because they crystallize much of what is so
lovable and amusing about Bottom. His overabundant self-confidence burbles out in his grandiose idea that although no one could
possibly understand his dream, it is worthy of being immortalized
in a poem. His tendency to make melodramatic rhetorical mistakes
manifests itself plentifully, particularly in his comically mixed-up
association of body parts and senses: he suggests that eyes can hear,
ears see, hands taste, tongues think, and hearts speak.

QUOTATIONS

5. If we shadows have offended,
    Think but this, and all is mended:
    That you have but slumbered here,
    While these visions did appear;
    And this weak and idle theme,
    No more yielding but a dream,
    Gentles, do not reprehend.
    If you pardon, we will mend.

Puck speaks these lines in an address to the audience near the end of *A Midsummer Night's Dream*, extending the theme of dreams beyond the world of the play and putting the reality of the audience's experience into question (V.epilogue.1–8). As many of the characters (Bottom and Theseus among them) believe that the magical events of the play's action were merely a dream, Puck tells the crowd that if the play has offended them, they too should remember it simply as a dream—"That you have but slumbered here, / While these visions did appear." The speech offers a commentary on the dreamlike atmosphere of *A Midsummer Night's Dream* and casts the play as a magical dream in which the audience shares.

QUOTATIONS

KEY FACTS

FULL TITLE
A Midsummer Night's Dream

AUTHOR
William Shakespeare

TYPE OF WORK
Play

GENRES
Comedy; fantasy; romance; farce

LANGUAGE
English

TIME AND PLACE WRITTEN
London, 1594 or 1595

DATE OF FIRST PUBLICATION
1600

PUBLISHER
Thomas Fisher

NARRATOR
None

CLIMAX
In the strictest sense, there is no real climax, as the conflicts of the play are all resolved swiftly by magical means in Act IV; the moment of greatest tension is probably the quarrel between the lovers in Act III, scene ii.

PROTAGONIST
Because there are three main groups of characters, there is no single protagonist in the play; however, Puck is generally considered the most important character.

ANTAGONIST
None; the play's tensions are mostly the result of circumstances, accidents, and mistakes.

SETTINGS (TIME)
Combines elements of Ancient Greece with elements of Renaissance England

SETTINGS (PLACE)
Athens and the forest outside its walls

POINT OF VIEW
Varies from scene to scene

FALLING ACTION
Act V, scene i, which centers on the craftsmen's play

TENSE
Present

FORESHADOWING
Comments made in Act I, scene i about the difficulties that lovers face

TONES
Romantic; comedic; fantastic; satirical; dreamlike; joyful; farcical

SYMBOLS
Theseus and Hippolyta represent order, stability, and wakefulness; Theseus's hounds represent the coming of morning; Oberon's love potion represents the power and instability of love.

THEMES
The difficulties of love; magic; the nature of dreams; the relationships between fantasy and reality and between environment and experience

MOTIFS
Love out of balance; contrast (juxtaposed opposites, such as beautiful and ugly, short and tall, clumsy and graceful, ethereal and earthy)

Study Questions

1. *Discuss the role of the play-within-a-play in Act V of A Midsummer Night's Dream. Does the Pyramus and Thisbe story have any relevance to the main story, or is it simply a comical interlude? What effect does the craftsmen's production of their play have on the tone of A Midsummer Night's Dream as a whole?*

The story of Pyramus and Thisbe offers a very subtle return to a couple of the main elements of *A Midsummer Night's Dream:* lovers caught up in misunderstanding and sorrow enhanced by the darkness of night. Like the main story of the outer play, the inner play consists of a tragic premise made comical by the actors. The craftsmen's unintentionally goofy portrayal of the woe of Pyramus and Thisbe makes the melodramatic romantic entanglements of the young Athenian lovers seem even more comical.

However, it is important to recognize as well that the inherent structure of a play-within-a-play allows Shakespeare to show off his talent by inserting a gem of pure comedy. The conflicts have been resolved and a happy ending procured for all; the performance, thus, has no impact on the plot. Rather, the craftsmen's hilarious bungling of the heavy tragedy allows the audience, and the melodramatic Athenian lovers, to laugh and take delight in the spectacle of the play.

2.   *How does the play's broad frame of reference heighten
     its use of contrast as an atmospheric device? More
     generally, how does Shakespeare use contrasting tones
     and characters in the play?*

That Shakespeare takes his characters from vastly different sources (e.g., the bumbling, rough craftsmen and the delicate, fanciful fairies) contributes to the imaginative scope and pervasive absurdity of *A Midsummer Night's Dream*. Shakespeare combines the contrasting elements of the play in startling and grotesque ways, as in the royal Titania's love for the ass-headed Bottom. He thus creates the sense that the normal rules and operations of reality have been suspended: if the magical Titania can fall in love with the ludicrous Bottom, anything can happen. The play's extraordinarily varied frame of reference, which includes elements of Greek mythology (Theseus and Hippolyta), aspects of the contemporary London theatrical tradition (males playing females in the craftsmen's play), characters of Babylonian origin (Pyramus and Thisbe) and from English fairy lore (Puck), and classical literary analogues (Titania and Oberon), adds to the surreal quality of the play by juxtaposing elements that clash stylistically.

3. *How is* A MIDSUMMER NIGHT'S DREAM *structured? Is there anything unusual in its treatment of the five-act dramatic form?*

A Midsummer Night's Dream fits into four acts all of the material that would normally occupy a five-act play; the main story, climax, and even a period of falling action are capped by a happy turn of events that would seem to mark the play's end. It is somewhat strange, then, that Shakespeare includes a fifth act. Since he has already resolved the tensions of the main plot, he treats Act V as a joyful comic epilogue. Except for a short closing scene, the act is committed wholly to the craftsmen's performance of *Pyramus and Thisbe*. In wrapping up the conflict before the last act, Shakespeare affords himself the opportunity to give the audience one act of pure, uncomplicated comedy. He offers a play-within-a-play whose comical rendition caps the cheerful mood of the Athenians watching the play.

How to Write
Literary Analysis

The Literary Essay: A Step-by-Step Guide

When you read for pleasure, your only goal is enjoyment. You might find yourself reading to get caught up in an exciting story, to learn about an interesting time or place, or just to pass time. Maybe you're looking for inspiration, guidance, or a reflection of your own life. There are as many different, valid ways of reading a book as there are books in the world.

When you read a work of literature in an English class, however, you're being asked to read in a special way: you're being asked to perform *literary analysis*. To analyze something means to break it down into smaller parts and then examine how those parts work, both individually and together. Literary analysis involves examining all the parts of a novel, play, short story, or poem—elements such as character, setting, tone, and imagery—and thinking about how the author uses those elements to create certain effects.

A literary essay isn't a book review: you're not being asked whether or not you liked a book or whether you'd recommend it to another reader. A literary essay also isn't like the kind of book report you wrote when you were younger, where your teacher wanted you to summarize the book's action. A high school- or college-level literary essay asks, "How does this piece of literature actually work?" "How does it do what it does?" and, "Why might the author have made the choices he or she did?"

The Seven Steps
No one is born knowing how to analyze literature; it's a skill you learn and a process you can master. As you gain more practice with this kind of thinking and writing, you'll be able to craft a method that works best for you. But until then, here are seven basic steps to writing a well-constructed literary essay:

1. Ask questions
2. Collect evidence
3. Construct a thesis

4. *Develop and organize arguments*
5. *Write the introduction*
6. *Write the body paragraphs*
7. *Write the conclusion*

---

1. ASK QUESTIONS

When you're assigned a literary essay in class, your teacher will often provide you with a list of writing prompts. Lucky you! Now all you have to do is choose one. Do yourself a favor and pick a topic that interests you. You'll have a much better (not to mention easier) time if you start off with something you enjoy thinking about. If you are asked to come up with a topic by yourself, though, you might start to feel a little panicked. Maybe you have too many ideas—or none at all. Don't worry. Take a deep breath and start by asking yourself these questions:

- **What struck you?** Did a particular image, line, or scene linger in your mind for a long time? If it fascinated you, chances are you can draw on it to write a fascinating essay.

- **What confused you?** Maybe you were surprised to see a character act in a certain way, or maybe you didn't understand why the book ended the way it did. Confusing moments in a work of literature are like a loose thread in a sweater: if you pull on it, you can unravel the entire thing. Ask yourself why the author chose to write about that character or scene the way he or she did and you might tap into some important insights about the work as a whole.

- **Did you notice any patterns?** Is there a phrase that the main character uses constantly or an image that repeats throughout the book? If you can figure out how that pattern weaves through the work and what the significance of that pattern is, you've almost got your entire essay mapped out.

- **Did you notice any contradictions or ironies?** Great works of literature are complex; great literary essays recognize and explain those complexities. Maybe the title (*Happy Days*) totally disagrees with the book's subject matter (hungry orphans dying in the woods). Maybe the main character acts one way around his family and a completely different way around his friends and associates. If you can find a way to explain a work's contradictory elements, you've got the seeds of a great essay.

At this point, you don't need to know exactly what you're going to say about your topic; you just need a place to begin your exploration. You can help direct your reading and brainstorming by formulating your topic as a *question,* which you'll then try to answer in your essay. The best questions invite critical debates and discussions, not just a rehashing of the summary. Remember, you're looking for something you can *prove or argue* based on evidence you find in the text. Finally, remember to keep the scope of your question in mind: is this a topic you can adequately address within the word or page limit you've been given? Conversely, is this a topic big enough to fill the required length?

Good Questions

"Are Romeo and Juliet's parents responsible for the deaths of their children?"
"Why do pigs keep showing up in Lord of the Flies?*"*
"Are Dr. Frankenstein and his monster alike? How?"

Bad Questions

"What happens to Scout in To Kill a Mockingbird?*"*
"What do the other characters in Julius Caesar *think about Caesar?"*
"How does Hester Prynne in The Scarlet Letter *remind me of my sister?"*

---

2. Collect Evidence

Once you know what question you want to answer, it's time to scour the book for things that will help you answer the question. Don't worry if you don't know what you want to say yet—right now you're just collecting ideas and material and letting it all percolate. Keep track of passages, symbols, images, or scenes that deal with your topic. Eventually, you'll start making connections between these examples and your thesis will emerge.

Here's a brief summary of the various parts that compose each and every work of literature. These are the elements that you will analyze in your essay, and which you will offer as evidence to support your arguments. For more on the parts of literary works, see the Glossary of Literary Terms at the end of this section.

ELEMENTS OF STORY These are the *what*s of the work—what happens, where it happens, and to whom it happens.

- **Plot:** All of the events and actions of the work.

- **Character:** The people who act and are acted upon in a literary work. The main character of a work is known as the *protagonist*.

- **Conflict:** The central tension in the work. In most cases, the protagonist wants something, while opposing forces (antagonists) hinder the protagonist's progress.

- **Setting:** When and where the work takes place. Elements of setting include location, time period, time of day, weather, social atmosphere, and economic conditions.

- **Narrator:** The person telling the story. The narrator may straightforwardly report what happens, convey the subjective opinions and perceptions of one or more characters, or provide commentary and opinion in his or her own voice.

- **Themes:** The main idea or message of the work—usually an abstract idea about people, society, or life in general. A work may have many themes, which may be in tension with one another.

ELEMENTS OF STYLE These are the *how*s—how the characters speak, how the story is constructed, and how language is used throughout the work.

- **Structure and organization:** How the parts of the work are assembled. Some novels are narrated in a linear, chronological fashion, while others skip around in time. Some plays follow a traditional three- or five-act structure, while others are a series of loosely connected scenes. Some authors deliberately leave gaps in their works, leaving readers to puzzle out the missing information. A work's structure and organization can tell you a lot about the kind of message it wants to convey.

- **Point of view:** The perspective from which a story is told. In *first-person point of view,* the narrator involves him or herself in the story. ("I went to the store"; "We watched in horror as the bird slammed into the window.") A first-person narrator is usually the protagonist of the work, but not always. In *third-person point of view,* the narrator does not participate in the story. A third-person narrator may closely follow a specific character, recounting that individual character's thoughts or experiences, or it may be what we call an *omniscient* narrator. Omniscient narrators see and know all: they can witness any event in any time or place and are privy to the inner thoughts and feelings of all characters. Remember that the narrator and the author are not the same thing!

- **Diction:** Word choice. Whether a character uses dry, clinical language or flowery prose with lots of exclamation points can tell you a lot about his or her attitude and personality.

- **Syntax:** Word order and sentence construction. Syntax is a crucial part of establishing an author's narrative voice. Ernest Hemingway, for example, is known for writing in very short, straightforward sentences, while James Joyce characteristically wrote in long, incredibly complicated lines.

- **Tone:** The mood or feeling of the text. Diction and syntax often contribute to the tone of a work. A novel written in short, clipped sentences that use small, simple words might feel brusque, cold, or matter-of-fact.

- **Imagery:** Language that appeals to the senses, representing things that can be seen, smelled, heard, tasted, or touched.

- **Figurative language:** Language that is not meant to be interpreted literally. The most common types of figurative language are *metaphors* and *similes,* which compare two unlike things in order to suggest a similarity between them— for example, "All the world's a stage," or "The moon is like a ball of green cheese." (Metaphors say one thing *is* another thing; similes claim that one thing is *like* another thing.)

3. CONSTRUCT A THESIS

When you've examined all the evidence you've collected and know how you want to answer the question, it's time to write your thesis statement. A *thesis* is a claim about a work of literature that needs to be supported by evidence and arguments. The thesis statement is the heart of the literary essay, and the bulk of your paper will be spent trying to prove this claim. A good thesis will be:

- **Arguable.** "*The Great Gatsby* describes New York society in the 1920s" isn't a thesis—it's a fact.

- **Provable through textual evidence**. "*Hamlet* is a confusing but ultimately very well-written play" is a weak thesis because it offers the writer's personal opinion about the book. Yes, it's arguable, but it's not a claim that can be proved or supported with examples taken from the play itself.

- **Surprising**. "Both George and Lenny change a great deal in *Of Mice and Men*" is a weak thesis because it's obvious. A really strong thesis will argue for a reading of the text that is not immediately apparent.

- **Specific**. "Dr. Frankenstein's monster tells us a lot about the human condition" is *almost* a really great thesis statement, but it's still too vague. What does the writer mean by "a lot"? *How* does the monster tell us so much about the human condition?

GOOD THESIS STATEMENTS

Question: In *Romeo and Juliet*, which is more powerful in shaping the lovers' story: fate or foolishness?

Thesis: "Though Shakespeare defines Romeo and Juliet as 'star-crossed lovers' and images of stars and planets appear throughout the play, a closer examination of that celestial imagery reveals that the stars are merely witnesses to the characters' foolish activities and not the causes themselves."

Question: How does the bell jar function as a symbol in Sylvia Plath's *The Bell Jar*?

Thesis: "A bell jar is a bell-shaped glass that has three basic uses: to hold a specimen for observation, to contain gases, and to maintain a vacuum. The bell jar appears in each of these capacities in *The Bell Jar*, Plath's semi-autobiographical novel, and each appearance marks a different stage in Esther's mental breakdown."

Question: Would Piggy in *Lord of the Flies* make a good island leader if he were given the chance?

Thesis: "Though the intelligent, rational, and innovative Piggy has the mental characteristics of a good leader, he ultimately lacks the social skills necessary to be an effective one. Golding emphasizes this point by giving Piggy a foil in the charismatic Jack, whose magnetic personality allows him to capture and wield power effectively, if not always wisely."

4. Develop and Organize Arguments

The reasons and examples that support your thesis will form the middle paragraphs of your essay. Since you can't really write your thesis statement until you know how you'll structure your argument, you'll probably end up working on steps 3 and 4 at the same time.

There's no single method of argumentation that will work in every context. One essay prompt might ask you to compare and contrast two characters, while another asks you to trace an image through a given work of literature. These questions require different kinds of answers and therefore different kinds of arguments. Below, we'll discuss three common kinds of essay prompts and some strategies for constructing a solid, well-argued case.

Types of Literary Essays

- **Compare and contrast**

  Compare and contrast the characters of Huck and Jim in The Adventures of Huckleberry Finn.

  Chances are you've written this kind of essay before. In an academic literary context, you'll organize your arguments the same way you would in any other class. You can either go *subject by subject* or *point by point*. In the former, you'll discuss one character first and then the second. In the latter, you'll choose several traits (attitude toward life, social status, images and metaphors associated with the character) and devote a paragraph to each. You may want to use a mix of these two approaches—for example, you may want to spend a paragraph a piece broadly sketching Huck's and Jim's personalities before transitioning into a paragraph or two that describes a few key points of comparison. This can be a highly effective strategy if you want to make a counterintuitive argument—that, despite seeming to be totally different, the two objects being compared are actually similar in a very important way (or vice versa). Remember that your essay should reveal something fresh or unexpected about the text, so think beyond the obvious parallels and differences.

- **Trace**

  Choose an image—for example, birds, knives, or eyes—and trace that image throughout Macbeth.

  Sounds pretty easy, right? All you need to do is read the play, underline every appearance of a knife in *Macbeth*, and then list them in your essay in the order they appear, right? Well, not exactly. Your teacher doesn't want a simple catalog of examples. He or she wants to see you make *connections* between those examples—that's the difference between summarizing and analyzing. In the *Macbeth* example above, think about the different contexts in which knives appear in the play and to what effect. In *Macbeth,* there are real knives and imagined knives; knives that kill and knives that simply threaten. Categorize and classify your examples to give them some order. Finally, always keep the overall effect in mind. After you choose and analyze your examples, you should come to some greater understanding about the work, as well as your chosen image, symbol, or phrase's role in developing the major themes and stylistic strategies of that work.

- **Debate**

  Is the society depicted in 1984 *good for its citizens?*

  In this kind of essay, you're being asked to debate a moral, ethical, or aesthetic issue regarding the work. You might be asked to judge a character or group of characters (*Is Caesar responsible for his own demise?*) or the work itself (*Is* JANE EYRE *a feminist novel?*). For this kind of essay, there are two important points to keep in mind. First, don't simply base your arguments on your personal feelings and reactions. Every literary essay expects you to read and analyze the work, so search for evidence in the text. What do characters in *1984* have to say about the government of Oceania? What images does Orwell use that might give you a hint about his attitude toward the government? As in any debate, you also need to make sure that you define all the necessary terms before you begin to argue your case. What does it mean to be a "good" society? What makes a novel "feminist"? You should define your terms right up front, in the first paragraph after your introduction.

  Second, remember that strong literary essays make contrary and surprising arguments. Try to think outside the box. In the *1984* example above, it seems like the obvious answer would be no, the totalitarian society depicted in Orwell's novel is *not* good for its citizens. But can you think of any arguments for the opposite side? Even if your final assertion is that the novel depicts a cruel, repressive, and therefore harmful society, acknowledging and responding to the counterargument will strengthen your overall case.

LITERARY ANALYSIS

5. WRITE THE INTRODUCTION

Your introduction sets up the entire essay. It's where you present your topic and articulate the particular issues and questions you'll be addressing. It's also where you, as the writer, introduce yourself to your readers. A persuasive literary essay immediately establishes its writer as a knowledgeable, authoritative figure.

An introduction can vary in length depending on the overall length of the essay, but in a traditional five-paragraph essay it should be no longer than one paragraph. However long it is, your introduction needs to:

- **Provide any necessary context.** Your introduction should situate the reader and let him or her know what to expect. What book are you discussing? Which characters? What topic will you be addressing?

- **Answer the "So what?" question.** Why is this topic important, and why is your particular position on the topic noteworthy? Ideally, your introduction should pique the reader's interest by suggesting how your argument is surprising or otherwise counterintuitive. Literary essays make unexpected connections and reveal less-than-obvious truths.

- **Present your thesis.** This usually happens at or very near the end of your introduction.

- **Indicate the shape of the essay to come.** Your reader should finish reading your introduction with a good sense of the scope of your essay as well as the path you'll take toward proving your thesis. You don't need to spell out every step, but you do need to suggest the organizational pattern you'll be using.

Your introduction should not:

- **Be vague.** Beware of the two killer words in literary analysis: *interesting* and *important*. Of course the work, question, or example is interesting and important—that's why you're writing about it!

- **Open with any grandiose assertions.** Many student readers think that beginning their essays with a flamboyant statement such as, "Since the dawn of time, writers have been fascinated with the topic of free will," makes them sound important and commanding. You know what? It actually sounds pretty amateurish.

- **Wildly praise the work.** Another typical mistake student writers make is extolling the work or author. Your teacher doesn't need to be told that "Shakespeare is perhaps the greatest writer in the English language." You can mention a work's reputation in passing—by referring to *The Adventures of Huckleberry Finn* as "Mark Twain's enduring classic," for example—but don't make a point of bringing it up unless that reputation is key to your argument.

- **Go off-topic.** Keep your introduction streamlined and to the point. Don't feel the need to throw in all kinds of bells and whistles in order to impress your reader—just get to the point as quickly as you can, without skimping on any of the required steps.

---

6. Write the Body Paragraphs

Once you've written your introduction, you'll take the arguments you developed in step 4 and turn them into your body paragraphs. The organization of this middle section of your essay will largely be determined by the argumentative strategy you use, but no matter how you arrange your thoughts, your body paragraphs need to do the following:

- **Begin with a strong topic sentence.** Topic sentences are like signs on a highway: they tell the reader where they are and where they're going. A good topic sentence not only alerts readers to what issue will be discussed in the following paragraph but also gives them a sense of what argument will be made *about* that issue. "Rumor and gossip play an important role in *The Crucible*" isn't a strong topic sentence because it doesn't tell us very much. "The community's constant gossiping creates an environment that allows false accusations to flourish" is a much stronger topic sentence— it not only tells us *what* the paragraph will discuss (gossip) but *how* the paragraph will discuss the topic (by showing how gossip creates a set of conditions that leads to the play's climactic action).

- **Fully and completely develop a single thought.** Don't skip around in your paragraph or try to stuff in too much material. Body paragraphs are like bricks: each individual one needs to be strong and sturdy or the entire structure will collapse. Make sure you have really proven your point before moving on to the next one.

- **Use transitions effectively.** Good literary essay writers know that each paragraph must be clearly and strongly linked to the material around it. Think of each paragraph as a response to the one that precedes it. Use transition words and phrases such as *however, similarly, on the contrary, therefore,* and *furthermore* to indicate what kind of response you're making.

7. WRITE THE CONCLUSION
Just as you used the introduction to ground your readers in the topic before providing your thesis, you'll use the conclusion to quickly summarize the specifics learned thus far and then hint at the broader implications of your topic. A good conclusion will:

- **Do more than simply restate the thesis.** If your thesis argued that *The Catcher in the Rye* can be read as a Christian allegory, don't simply end your essay by saying, "And that is why *The Catcher in the Rye* can be read as a Christian allegory." If you've constructed your arguments well, this kind of statement will just be redundant.

- **Synthesize the arguments, not summarize them.** Similarly, don't repeat the details of your body paragraphs in your conclusion. The reader has already read your essay, and chances are it's not so long that they've forgotten all your points by now.

- **Revisit the "So what?" question.** In your introduction, you made a case for why your topic and position are important. You should close your essay with the same sort of gesture. What do your readers know now that they didn't know before? How will that knowledge help them better appreciate or understand the work overall?

- **Move from the specific to the general.** Your essay has most likely treated a very specific element of the work—a single character, a small set of images, or a particular passage. In your conclusion, try to show how this narrow discussion has wider implications for the work overall. If your essay on *To Kill a Mockingbird* focused on the character of Boo Radley, for example, you might want to include a bit in your conclusion about how he fits into the novel's larger message about childhood, innocence, or family life.

- **Stay relevant.** Your conclusion should suggest new directions of thought, but it shouldn't be treated as an opportunity to pad your essay with all the extra, interesting ideas you came up with during your brainstorming sessions but couldn't fit into the essay proper. Don't attempt to stuff in unrelated queries or too many abstract thoughts.

- **Avoid making overblown closing statements.** A conclusion should open up your highly specific, focused discussion, but it should do so without drawing a sweeping lesson about life or human nature. Making such observations may be part of the point of reading, but it's almost always a mistake in essays, where these observations tend to sound overly dramatic or simply silly.

A+ Essay Checklist

Congratulations! If you've followed all the steps we've outlined above, you should have a solid literary essay to show for all your efforts. What if you've got your sights set on an A+? To write the kind of superlative essay that will be rewarded with a perfect grade, keep the following rubric in mind. These are the qualities that teachers expect to see in a truly A+ essay. How does yours stack up?

- ✓ Demonstrates a thorough understanding of the book
- ✓ Presents an original, compelling argument
- ✓ Thoughtfully analyzes the text's formal elements
- ✓ Uses appropriate and insightful examples
- ✓ Structures ideas in a logical and progressive order
- ✓ Demonstrates a mastery of sentence construction, transitions, grammar, spelling, and word choice

LITERARY ANALYSIS

SUGGESTED ESSAY TOPICS

1. *Though Bottom often steals the show in performance, Puck is usually considered the most important character in* A MIDSUMMER NIGHT'S DREAM. *Comparing Puck to Bottom, why might Puck be considered the protagonist? In what way does Puck's spirit dominate the mood of the play? In what ways does the comedy surrounding Puck differ from that surrounding Bottom?*

2. *Compare and contrast the Athenian lovers with the craftsmen. In what ways are the dispositions of the two groups different from each other? Are they the same in any way?*

3. *What role do Theseus and Hippolyta play in* A MIDSUMMER NIGHT'S DREAM? *What is the significance of the fact that they are absent from the play's main action?*

4. *It has been argued that the characters of the Athenian lovers are not particularly differentiated from one another—that Hermia is quite like Helena (even down to her name) and that Demetrius resembles Lysander. Do you think that this is the case, or do you think that the lovers emerge as individuals? If you believe that these characters are quite similar to one another, what do you think Shakespeare's intent was in making them so?*

LITERARY ANALYSIS

A+ Student Essay

Many people have categorized *A Midsummer Night's Dream* as a romantic comedy. How accurate is this assessment?

A Midsummer Night's Dream, one of Shakespeare's most beloved comedies, is generally thought of as a sparkling romantic farce. However, while the play is lovely and comic, it also has a strong trace of darkness and cruelty, a sinister underside that is inextricable from its amorous themes. *Midsummer* may end with a series of happy weddings, but along the way it clearly depicts how male-female relationships can involve a great amount of cruelty, with the potential to spread discord throughout society.

Nearly all the male characters threaten their female counterparts with violence at some point in the play. Theseus, for example, won Hippolyta not through seduction or courtship but by military conquest, having vanquished the Amazons, her tribe of woman warriors. He says to her in the opening scene, "I wooed thee with my sword, / And won thy love doing thee injuries," drawing an explicit connection between love and assault. Later in the same scene, Egeus publicly threatens to kill Hermia, his daughter, if she does not consent to marry Demetrius. Oberon, for his part, does not put Titania at risk of true physical danger, but he does brainwash her with a love-potion for the express purpose of humiliating and humbling her. Lysander may be the only male who does not consciously seek to harm his mate. But even so, Hermia cannot escape peril. Just after the bewitched Lysander abandons her, she wakes from a nightmare, trembling with fear as she describes how she dreamt she saw "a serpent [eat her] heart away." Though Lysander isn't in control of his own actions at this moment, Hermia's subconscious still registers his desertion as an act of violation.

The female characters in the play, particularly Helena and Hermia, end up internalizing much of this violent behavior. In the most vicious exchange in the play, Lysander bluntly tells the lovesick Helena that he does not love her and that he is "sick" when he looks at her. He warns her that he will "do [her] mischief" in the woods—a far more menacing promise when we realize that *mischief* had a much stronger connotation in the period, meaning something closer to "harm" or "evil" than "naughtiness." Helena, however,

LITERARY ANALYSIS

is undeterred. She accepts the aggression directed at her and turns it into an argument for her stamina, pleading with him to treat her like his "spaniel," since the more he "beat[s]" her, the more she will "fawn" on him. Eventually, the two young women fall victim to the hostility in the air and turn on one another. Their confrontation in Act III, scene ii is often played as a comic catfight, but that ignores the poignancy of Helena's speech, in which she pleads with her "sister" not to "rend [their] ancient love asunder" by conspiring with the men to shame her. Hermia, however, does not listen, and the two dissolve into a torrent of mutual abuse. Even at the end of the play, when the couples are paired off harmoniously, it is unclear whether the women's intimate friendship will ever be repaired.

Throughout the play, romantic strife is portrayed as a force that can spread, like a contagion. At one point, the whole earth becomes infected. When the sparring fairy monarchs, Titania and Oberon, confront each other in Act II, scene i, Titania describes a tumultuous world filled with sickly clouds and rotting vegetation. She insists that this chaos has sprung from her and Oberon's quarrel, and that they are the "parents" of the planet's current state of turmoil.

A Midsummer Night's Dream ends with several happy (if magically-induced) weddings, but even the joy of the closing celebration does not completely banish the play's threatening undercurrent. The nuptials are commemorated with a clownish performance, but significantly, the craftsmen's theme is a gruesome one: a romantic couple that meets a violent and tragic end. In addition, the blessings offered by Puck and Oberon seem to evoke more terror than good will. Oberon offers the more traditional blessing, wishing the couples fertility and lasting love. However, he also mentions "blots of nature," such as harelips and other deformities, calling attention to the dangers that can befall vulnerable children even as he wards them away. Puck, for his part, spends most of his speech describing all the horrible things that lurk outside the wedding chamber door, such as hungry lions and ghosts from "gaping" graves. In the end, we don't know if the newlyweds are inside experiencing the flush of matrimonial bliss or if the discord that has been bubbling up throughout the play has unsettled them: As Puck closes the door against the terrible creatures of the night, he shuts the audience out, as well. With the ultimate fate of our protagonists so ambiguous, *A Midsummer Night's Dream* cannot properly be called a romantic comedy.

Glossary of Literary Terms

ANTAGONIST

The entity that acts to frustrate the goals of the *protagonist*. The antagonist is usually another *character* but may also be a non-human force.

ANTIHERO / ANTIHEROINE

A *protagonist* who is not admirable or who challenges notions of what should be considered admirable.

CHARACTER

A person, animal, or any other thing with a personality that appears in a *narrative*.

CLIMAX

The moment of greatest intensity in a text or the major turning point in the *plot*.

CONFLICT

The central struggle that moves the *plot* forward. The conflict can be the *protagonist*'s struggle against fate, nature, society, or another person.

FIRST-PERSON POINT OF VIEW

A literary style in which the *narrator* tells the story from his or her own *point of view* and refers to himself or herself as "I." The narrator may be an active participant in the story or just an observer.

HERO / HEROINE

The principal *character* in a literary work or *narrative*.

IMAGERY

Language that brings to mind sense-impressions, representing things that can be seen, smelled, heard, tasted, or touched.

MOTIF

A recurring idea, structure, contrast, or device that develops or informs the major *themes* of a work of literature.

NARRATIVE

A story.

NARRATOR

The person (sometimes a *character*) who tells a story; the *voice* assumed by the writer. The narrator and the author of the work of literature are not the same person.

PLOT

The arrangement of the events in a story, including the sequence in which they are told, the relative emphasis they are given, and the causal connections between events.

POINT OF VIEW

The *perspective* that a *narrative* takes toward the events it describes.

PROTAGONIST

The main *character* around whom the story revolves.

SETTING

The location of a *narrative* in time and space. Setting creates mood or atmosphere.

SUBPLOT

A secondary *plot* that is of less importance to the overall story but may serve as a point of contrast or comparison to the main plot.

SYMBOL

An object, *character,* figure, or color that is used to represent an abstract idea or concept. Unlike an *emblem,* a symbol may have different meanings in different contexts.

SYNTAX

The way the words in a piece of writing are put together to form lines, phrases, or clauses; the basic structure of a piece of writing.

THEME

A fundamental and universal idea explored in a literary work.

TONE

The author's attitude toward the subject or *characters* of a story or poem or toward the reader.

VOICE

An author's individual way of using language to reflect his or her own personality and attitudes. An author communicates voice through *tone, diction,* and *syntax.*

LITERARY ANALYSIS

A Note on Plagiarism

Plagiarism—presenting someone else's work as your own—rears its ugly head in many forms. Many students know that copying text without citing it is unacceptable. But some don't realize that even if you're not quoting directly, but instead are paraphrasing or summarizing, *it is plagiarism* unless you cite the source.

Here are the most common forms of plagiarism:

- Using an author's phrases, sentences, or paragraphs without citing the source
- Paraphrasing an author's ideas without citing the source
- Passing off another student's work as your own

How do you steer clear of plagiarism? You should *always* acknowledge all words and ideas that aren't your own by using quotation marks around verbatim text or citations like footnotes and endnotes to note another writer's ideas. For more information on how to give credit when credit is due, ask your teacher for guidance or visit www.sparknotes.com.

Review & Resources

Quiz

1. Who is chosen to play the lion in the craftsmen's play?

    A. Bottom
    B. Quince
    C. Peaseblossom
    D. Snug

2. Which of the young Athenians is first affected by the love potion?

    A. Lysander
    B. Helena
    C. Hermia
    D. Demetrius

3. Which man does Hermia's father want her to marry?

    A. Lysander
    B. Demetrius
    C. Theseus
    D. Philostrate

4. Where do Lysander and Hermia plan to be married?

    A. Theseus's palace
    B. Lysander's aunt's house
    C. The temple of Diana
    D. A forest glade

5. What part of her appearance does Hermia believe Helena has exploited to win Lysander's love?

    A. Her hair
    B. Her face
    C. Her height
    D. Her legs

6. What does Oberon want that Titania refuses to give him?

Λ. Her attendant, an Indian prince
B. Her magic wand
C. Her maid-in-waiting
D. Her love

7. Why does Pyramus, in the craftsmen's play, kill himself?

A. Thisbe does not love him.
B. Thisbe has been killed by a lion.
C. Thisbe has been killed by her father.
D. Pyramus *believes* Thisbe has been killed by a lion because he finds her tattered garment at their meeting place.

8. Who brings the complaint against Hermia to Theseus in Act I?

A. Egeus
B. Bottom
C. Hippolyta
D. Demetrius

9. Of whom is Hippolyta the queen?

A. The Pygmies
B. The Centaurs
C. The Amazons
D. The Babylonians

10. How does Puck prevent Demetrius and Lysander from fighting?

A. By freezing them
B. By transforming their weapons to weeds
C. By squeezing the love potion onto their eyelids
D. By mimicking their voices and causing each to get lost in a separate part of the forest

REVIEW & RESOURCES

11. Which of the women is afraid of fighting?

    A. Hippolyta
    B. Hermia
    C. Titania
    D. Helena

12. Whom does Demetrius love at the end of the play?

    A. Titania
    B. Hippolyta
    C. Helena
    D. Hermia

13. With whom does Titania fall in love in Act III?

    A. Snug
    B. Puck
    C. Bottom
    D. Mustardseed

14. What prank does Puck play on Bottom?

    A. He transforms him into a bear.
    B. He steals his clothes.
    C. He changes his voice into that of a wood thrush.
    D. He changes his head into that of an ass.

15. Who first thinks of using the love potion on Titania?

    A. Puck
    B. Oberon
    C. Bottom
    D. Cobweb

16. Who speaks with Titania's quartet of attendants?

    A. None of the human characters
    B. All of the human characters
    C. Only Demetrius and Lysander
    D. Only Bottom

17. Why is the flower whose juice Oberon seeks special?

    A.   Titania has kissed it.
    B.   One of Cupid's arrows struck it.
    C.   It was a traditional symbol of love in English folklore.
    D.   Fairies sleep in it.

18. Which of the craftsmen is in charge of the rehearsals?

    A.   Quince
    B.   Snout
    C.   Bottom
    D.   Starveling

19. In what year was Shakespeare born?

    A.   1563
    B.   1616
    C.   1564
    D.   1615

20. Who tells Demetrius that Lysander and Hermia are planning to elope?

    A.   Hermia
    B.   Flute
    C.   Puck
    D.   Helena

21. What food does Bottom crave after Puck's mischief?

    A.   Steak
    B.   Kidney pie
    C.   Squirrel
    D.   Hay

22. What are Theseus and Hippolyta about to do before they discover the sleeping lovers?

    A.   Listen to Theseus's hounds baying.
    B.   Watch Theseus's falcons hunting.
    C.   Watch Theseus's deer roaming.
    D.   See Theseus's golden lion.

23. How many weddings take place before the play-within-a-play?

    A. 4
    B. 2
    C. 3
    D. 1

24. Who blesses Theseus and Hippolyta with a magical charm at the end of the play?

    A. Puck
    B. Oberon
    C. Titania
    D. Oberon and Titania

25. Who suggests that the audience consider whether the entire play has been a dream?

    A. Snout
    B. Puck
    C. Titania
    D. Peaseblossom

ANSWER KEY

1: D; 2: A; 3: B; 4: B; 5: C; 6: C; 7: D; 8: A; 9: C; 10: D; 11: D; 12: C;
13: C; 14: D; 15: B; 16: D; 17: B; 18: A; 19: C; 20: D; 21: D; 22: A;
23: C; 24: D; 25: B

Suggestions for Further Reading

BARBER, CESAR LOMBARDI. *Shakespeare's Festive Comedy: A Study of Dramatic Form and Its Relation to Social Custom.* Princeton, NJ: Princeton University Press, 1972.

BONAZZA, BLAZE O. *Shakespeare's Early Comedies: A Structural Analysis.* The Hague: Mouton, 1966.

BRIGGS, KATHARINE M. *The Anatomy of Puck.* London: Routledge & Kegan Paul, 1959.

FOAKES, R. A., ed. *A Midsummer Night's Dream.* Cambridge: Cambridge University Press, 2003.

KEHLER, DOROTHEA, ed. A MIDSUMMER NIGHT'S DREAM: *Critical Essays.* New York: Garland, 2001.

NEVO, RUTH. *Comic Transformations in Shakespeare.* New York: Routledge, reprint edition 2005.

RHOADES, DUANE. *Shakespeare's Defense of Poetry:* A MIDSUMMER NIGHT'S DREAM *and* THE TEMPEST. Westport, CT: Greenwood Press, 1986.

THOMPSON, STEPHEN P. *Readings on* A MIDSUMMER NIGHT'S DREAM. San Diego, CA: Greenhaven Press, 2000.

YOUNG, DAVID. *Something of Great Constancy: The Art of* A MIDSUMMER NIGHT'S DREAM. New Haven, CT: Yale University Press, 1966.

REVIEW & RESOURCES

SparkNotes Literature Guides

Visit sparknotes.com for many more!